When The Soul Sings

Dr. Pragya Mathur Kumar

BookLeaf Publishing

India | USA | UK

Made with ❤ on the BookLeaf Publishing Platform
www.bookleafpub.in
www.bookleafpub.com

Dedication

With lots of love, respect and gratitude to the wonderful
people who will always be a precious part of my life...
My home team
Dr.Prakhar Kumar, Prabhav & Prabhas
My parents
Ma (Mrs.Prabha Mathur) Papa (Dr.K.M.Mathur)
My in laws
Ma(Mrs.Mithilesh Kumar) Papa(Dr.Pramod Kumar).

Preface

The written word has been my friend for as long as I can remember.Growing up in a home where books were as important as food and sat smugly on the dining table at all times,writing came easily to me.

It started with school magazine articles and poems.I would scribble quotable quotes in a diary to decorate my essays with.Just like Papa ,I began to compile my own notes while reading and soon realised they were like a nursery of ideas with potential for growing into full fledged articles.I also saw Ma ,writing her thoughts and weaving stories around real life events.Her courage to share the deepest human experiences and emotions made me realise the power of sharing through writing.So many who read her stories identified with the characters and their journeys.When Papa wrote articles /essays/books,he would ask us to read through and edit them.As I grew up, I realised the magnitude and impact of the simple task he assigned to us .We fell in love with process of writing and polishing the content till it became its own best version.What I now find overwhelming also,is the ease with which he treated school going kids as editors for his brilliant writing.My sister Shikha and brother Shubhang have been my best buddies and cheerleaders throughout the milestones of my journey as a writer.Their spouses,Niraj Jijaji and Nandita also joined the club in time.I'm grateful and blessed for the support and encouragement from my in laws too,Dr.Pramod Kumar and Mrs.Mithilesh Kumar. There are no words to express my gratitude to my family,my home team.They became my anchors and my wings.Without their constant support,encouragement and appreciation ,the urge to write would not have flourished.While Prakhar,Prabhav,Prabhas often bore the brunt of sudden disappearances to complete a work in progress,they never complained.I'm blessed to have such a supportive team that let me be when self expression needed words to be written down.Above all,I'm grateful to the Divine Mother for inspiring me to record the songs my soul sings...

Acknowledgements

To everyone who has been part of my journey
To everyone who made me smile
To everyone who held my hand
To everyone who made me dance
To everyone who wiped my tears
Or helped me overcome my fears
To those who watched me from the banks
This heartfelt note is here to say...many thanks.

A special note of gratitude...to Bookleaf Publishing for the opportunity to publish When the Soul Sings.

1. Of Blossoming...in time

The seed fell through deep under the dirt,
The shell perhaps was really hurt
And then emerged a tiny green,
A sprout much stronger than the lonely seed alone had
been.
Through the surface emerged tender greens
And roots took root deep within.
Trickling drops of water held it close
The sun smiled,the wind danced
And then it rose.
A new beginning,a happy start
To a different life...of blossoming at last.
For the first time ever ,patience and hope brought joy
For in their own time,at their own pace...
Without being part of any rat race
Beautiful flowers blossomed in the same place
Which was at one time an unknown space.

2. Honey bee

In the vast universe
There exist
Many a tiny bee
With the wisdom and skill to know
How to make sweet honey....
How do they know
Exactly where to go
And what to pick and choose
Clear winners the bees emerge
With really nothing to lose.
Everything is perfect
There's really nothing wrong...
Mother Nature needs no campaigning...
She the very best,hands down.
If only humans could understand
This lesson from the bees
To take a little and then move on
Sharing with different shapes and form
There's no element of greed
All she takes is what she needs.
If we had half the "knowledge "
That guides the tiny bee

This earth would be a planet
That aliens would envy!!

3. The Bond Beyond

Surrounded by trees ,
Enveloped in cool breeze
Were some gurus and shishyas
Keeping a classical tradition alive .
The sound of the music and rhythmic beats
Made the temple of learning
A beautiful retreat.
As she entered the stage ,with folded hands
There was a silence of reverence among those in the
stands.
She spoke in a soft voice and introduced her piece
Then the magic unfolded as she danced to the beats.
Her movements were fluid
She moved with grace
Suddenly there was an aura surrounding her face.
Her eyes became brighter than the lights around
As she swirled to the melody of the soulful sound.
In a flash she was Yashoda ,full of love divine...
Admonishing little Kanha for stealing butter out of line.
When she smiled ,they all were smiling too
For the audience became one with the dancer in time.
The boundaries had melted like butter in the sun
When she performed soulfully...the Madhurashtakam.

Some were wiping away tears that flowed on and on
Her expressions of Bhakti had become their own
She had surpassed the barriers
Of time and space
Bringing everyone together
in a mystical embrace
To experience the magic
Of a bond beyond.

4. Ice cream for all

The warm summer breeze,
Tickled the leaves
Happy little children ,
Danced in the streets
It was holiday time for all the kids
And the Ice cream wallah was a real big hit!
Every evening he's come around
With the jingling bell's familiar sound
And much like the Pied Piper of Hamelin
All the little children would follow him
He'd open his matka -that was full of kulfi
And would sell his ice cream for a couple of rupees.
Melting ice and smacking lips
All the children loved his regular evening trips.

Grandma Ice cream ,screamed the little fellow
And rushed full speed to the cart below.
Here ,here my son-is your kulfi for today
Grabbing his birth right -he just walked away.
She stood there too...his young sister
Waiting to get a kulfi that was meant for her
Grandma ,I want one kulfi too
Like the one you just bought for dear Nanu.
With a shrug and a frown

Grandma turned around
And walked away from the jingling sound.

Soon after ,
One could see ,
Tthe tearful face
Of the sweet little girl
Who did not receive
An equal share of grace.
She looked at her brother -enjoying the treat
Her eyes told the story of a silent retreat.
She stared blankly -at the melting ice cream
For her that treat was a distant dream.
For she was an unwanted daughter and would bring no
gain
Was it her destiny...to learn and hide her pain?

I am sure when she sleeps and her dreams are on call
Somewhere there is a world
with ice cream for all.

5. A Gift Divine

The sun shone and smiled through the dancing trees
A golden glimmer of hope and peace
Of gifts manifold and promises
Bringing along untold mysteries.
Some happy some sad
Some sweet some sour
A bagful of many long and short stories.

At the break of dawn when the birds sing a song
There's a silent prayer unheard
May the days bring peace
Good health and happy times
May the earth be filled with musical rhymes
May the flowers grow bright and beautiful.

As the rising sun comes home to us
Sprinkling along glitters of glorious light
May we cherish the minutes,the hours each day
Before it sets and has gone away
To return tomorrow with the same sunshine
As much yours as it is mine.
A priceless treasure ,a gift divine.

6. Crimson Magic

It seemed as if the clouds were on fire
Splattering of crimson
Rising higher and higher
Till the sky smiled through
A serene shade of blue
Turning the crimson into a much lighter hue.
And suddenly it burst forth and shone
That big ball of fire which travels alone
Dismissing the night and dewdrops that fall
Like a cosmic pyre consuming it all.
Silently it comes and goes
The world still sleeps and hardly anyone knows
Except for the birds chirping merrily
Playing their part full of mirth and glee
They seem to tell the sleeping world
Wake up and watch
The magic unfurl.

7. Sunshine and rainbow too

He waited patiently for her to turn around
Oh his heart beat was loud
Perhaps even others could hear the sound
Slowly however
His tearful eyes shifted to the ground.

She couldn't look back
For she knew she had to go
There was really no choice
And he too would have to know
She was doing it for him
To watch him bloom and grow.

His cold little hands wiped the flowing tears
Stifling his sobs so no one hears
He stood alone in a world unknown
For the love of his life
Was gone...

It took many years for him to find
The value of what she had in mind
When she let go to give him wings
To help him learn his own song to sing
The roots have grown deep and strong

When he walks the hilly road
He can feel her coming along.

In the toughest moments of his life so far
She had always been the anchor even from afar
Now he made her proud as he stood tall
The seasons had changed
It was time for fall.

She heard the doorbell and turned to find
It was a fig of imagination of her monkey mind
Did he still remember that she'd left him and gone
Walking away from him without turning around?
She wished she could explain to him
How tough ,for her,it all had been.

Just then she heard a real loud knock
Or was it the big clock going tick tock?
With hope giving her tired feet speed
She rushed to open the wooden door
He stood there with a bouquet in hand
And a golden gift ...really grand.

Their eyes met and she could feel herself melt
For he had come home to her when it mattered most
Happy Valentine's Day...sweet Mother of mine
I know how much you cared to have left me behind

You are my sunshine and rainbow too
My heart will beat forever for you.

8. Let go

Thankfully ,it is in our power to choose
To let go that which is no longer of any use.
That one memory which still hurts and causes pain
Brings back a sense of loss,really nothing to gain.
Why not choose to embrace the new
Which brings along hope and promises too.
Like a river that flows trusting its path
Dancing along
Onward it goes.
What lies ahead
It really never knows
Crossing the hurdles along the way
It moves along each new day
Letting go of what was or could have been
Towards a tomorrow
Unknown unseen.
Driven along by the waves within
Choosing to flow
Choosing to let go.

9. Fleeting Life.

Transient
The days and nights
The lovely songs are too...
For none will last
Beyond their time
However good the reason or rhyme.
Bitter sweet... sometimes sour
Life goes by....hour by hour.
The minutes fly
The stream flows by
Some watchful eyes
Twinkle and smile
Every footstep
Making up the mile.
Crossroads...
Choices....
We make each day
Mapping out our journeys
Along the way.
The trees are watching
Be mindful of the steps
Roots know not
How far we have tread.
Closer to the truth

Unravelling mysteries
Gifting happiness
Dispelling misery
Nothing travels into the beyond
Dancing footprints
Are all that's left behind....
Sands passing through palms
Leaving a speck or two of gold
Pass on the joy
Feel it within
Until one day
The curtains close
Leaving images
Striking the pose
Infinite...immeasurable
Melting, merging,becoming whole.
©drpragyamathur@arunimankura

10. A bond with thunder

Walking in the park
After a dark and rainy night
I chanced upon
A truly moving sight.
A lovely looking snail
Was sliding along the path
In a slow and fluid motion
And no hurry at all.
While the walkers around
Even counted the number of steps
This marvel of Mother Nature
Had nothing to do with the rest.
For it was happy covering inches
Oblivious of the miles
Inspiring me to stop and watch
its journey with a smile.
Some would say it was slow
Some would say rather lazy
But the snail didn't need to know
Even if the world thought it was crazy.
Was it smelling the soothing fragrance
Of earth meeting tiny raindrops?
Was it aware it was inspiring
Someone to write a song?

Did the snail have any clue
Someone was tracking its move?
Where was it trying to go
What was it trying to do?
None of it seemed to matter
In that one moment of time
The snail perhaps knew better
Believing ...the universe is mine...
Where was it until yesterday
When the earth was dry and there was no rain?
How did it emerge out of nowhere
To share the path ...watered by the rain?
The more I think
The more I wonder
Is there a deeper bond
Between the snail and thunder?

11. Say Yes to life

Dear Students
Let no numbers ever have the power
To tell you what a failure you are
Let no person ever have the might
To make you feel that nothing you do is right.
Let no moment ever drag you down
Steal your smiles and make you frown.
You came to this world as a lovely little gift
Peep into your heart if your mind seems to drift
You will see the loving faces of people who hold you close.
No numbers can ever measure
That which the human bond knows
Since time unknown till eternity
The river of life just flows.
Hold on be strong ...focus on what you can do.
Build yourself up,one step at a time
Have confidence and hold your ground
The universe echoes with energy unbound.
Let the storm pass...for soon or late,it will.
Don't ever give up
In the middle of all the strife
You are a precious powerhouse
Say Yes to life.

12. Eternal glory

That day still comes
Once every year
Which was cause for celebration
The birthday of one so dear.
It brings many a simple memory
Gently unfolding like a flower
For the bond never ever weakens
Even with every passing hour...

It brings the memory of a beautiful soul
On a spiritual journey,with peace eternal as its goal.
Of a brief stopover that touched many lives
And changed them for the better
With innocent happy smiles.
Of a fleeting earthly visit
To be cherished forever in the hearts ...
Of those who loved the precious one
The purest bundle of joy ,from the start

With the brightest twinkling pair of eyes
Who surmounted tough challenges
And overcame the troublesome miles
Whose warm embrace would melt the heart
As would his naughty smile

Who was born to be a gift for all
But left too soon...while really small.

He was perhaps a chosen one
Not meant for the rat race
A gift of love, a blessing for all
Born of divine grace.
A special corner in our hearts,
Will always shine for him
Enveloped in glory eternal ...
Beyond the end or beginning in time.

13. Some fly ,some sing

Hope beckons
As the lone bird watches and
A warm glow glistens
across the horizon
Through the dark clouds.

Is it enough to stay a silent witness
Holding within
Faith and the promise of strong wings?
Or must it fly
And discover itself
By reaching out
To the vast blue sky?

What the bird will choose to do
No one can tell.
Deep down there also is
A merry chirpy song
The notes are all in tandem
The tune is nearly done...
What happens to the melody
That's waiting to be sung?
As the vast unknown beckons
The lone bird must decide

To reveal its hidden talent
Or just keep in locked inside.

Freedom to fly and freedom to sing
That's what every morning brings
And then it is
To each their own
Embracing the drift
Of the gust of wind
That carries along
Whatever lies within...
Some birds have sung...while others have flown
Exploring the beauty of the vast unknown.

14. A Little White Flower

Sometimes ...a little white flower
Perfect and pure
Becomes a reminder of someone you knew.
Of someone who lives in one part of your heart
Loved deeply,forever.
Bringing a smile
On a rainy day
A gift from the heavens
Calming through the storm
Soothing like balm
Making you realise
Even when you can't see them with your eyes
They are walking with you...alongside.

And then you smile
Knowing a deeper truth
There really is no going away...
For that which appears as the flower today
Was the tiny bud until yesterday
It all keeps miving ,changing forms
Embracing you through the cycles of time
Where everything melts into oneness
And nothing remains yours or mine.
And then you know...

It will only take a while
To be together again
Beyond this space and time.
Grateful for the moment
When it all became so clear
That which appears distant
May be somewhere really near...
And to think that all it took
Was a little white flower
Standing up to the big bright sun
The force of life for everyone.
All thanks again
To a little white flower
That had me in an embrace
For the tiniest part of an hour
In that fleeting second
When we came face to face
Life no longer remained a finite race.

15. Of Saplings and trees

Once upon a time
There was a small seed
It fell from the tree
Into the earth beneath.
The earth enveloped it in her womb
And the clouds above gave it nourishment
A tiny sapling then appeared
As days went by it grew
The baby leaves had a lovely hue
The brand new plant looked skyward and thought
"Much greater heights is what it sought.
But then alas!
It realised
The tree was large and with all its might
Would catch the rays of the glowing sun
And no sunlight could reach the plant
In a few days time...it died and was out of sight .

If those who are big and powerful
Don't let the sunlight reach below
How in the world will they find a place
And how will the tiny saplings grow?

But there is hope in the world

Somewhere someday
The little sapling will have its way
And it will bring along
Its own sunshine
And become more precious than a gold mine.
There will be a dream
And someone to say
Grow tall be strong
Go have your way.
Never mind that big old tree
It's far too proud and will soon fall you'll see.

You will grow your own roots and branches too
The winds will give you wings to soar
The cycle of life keeps moving along
You too will become a tree someday
What's yours will surely come your way...
For in the seed are many a tree
Waiting their turn
To be set free.

16. The Black Sheep

She was a little girl
Sweet and fair
Big bright eyes
Very curly hair
Growing up under the golden sun
She was full of life
A bundle of fun.

Then it was time
To go to school
Wihout an education
She'd be a fool
Not knowing to count
To read or write
Her future would be
Like a moonless night.

So off she went
To the hilltop school
In dark grey tunic
And clean cream shirt
With a bright red tie
She thought was really cool.

That was the start of a roller coster ride
With a teacher who made her wish she could hide.
She seemed to hate kids
And spoke in a rude loud tone
The little girl wished
She could just fly home....

This Miss was harsh and strict
Unforgiving too
And somehow seemed to think
Her class was adult too
No questions asked
None answered thereof
She assumed they'd learnt
Whatever she taught.

The little girl with curly hair
Got a taste that life was not always fair
Well , she wanted to know
Why we couldn't see
The lines on the globe
Drawn longitudinally?
How were we to believe they did exist
When the equator and tropics
Weren't visible in our midst?

There were too many questions

But she was afraid to ask
Because the Miss would have taken
Her to task
And rattled on in her usual grouse
Calling the curly haired girl
The Black Sheep of the house.

It took her a while to even figure out
What being a Black Sheep was all about.
It broke her heart
She could feel the pain
Miss had the power
To make tears rain.

She stopped speaking up
And pushed the questions aside
The curious voice in her
Eventually died.
Though the grown up Miss didn't even realise
She had shown the class
Not everyone was nice.

The 'Black Sheep' was lucky
To grow up in a home
Where words were used to heal
And not hurt anyone
Where she was free to ask

And free to err
And free to fly
With her dreams
Up in the air!

So she chose to become
A teacher who knew
The power of words
And how children grew
How every child was a miracle
And a blessing that was
Unique and special.

The world needs teachers
Who can use their power
Each day in school...every hour
To build not break
To heal not hurt
For the black sheep too
Can add some value to the world.

When the big bright eyes look up and see
A teacher who loves them and lets them be
A fine work in progress erring now and then
It's a dream run...that has just begun!

17. No beginning no end.

Contrary to how it may seem at first
Letting go is often beginning
Rather than the end.

For when the fruit is ripe and falls off the tree
It's the start of a seed's new journey
When the nest has been their home long enough
And their wings are ready for flight
It is time for her to let go and say bye
To the teeny meeny apples of her eye.

To seek and find their own destiny
They cross thresholds and go
For the seeds of many a beginning
Lie in the lap of letting go.

So many forms so many lives
Being born to grow and die
The cycle goes on and on and on
Visible to the Cosmic Eye.
There is no beginning
There is no end
Life is happening forever

Just across the bend.

18. Footprints

She followed the footprints
Out to the sea
Feeling the sand tickle
The sole of her feet

He was walking ahead
As if showing her the way
And yet turning around
To make sure she was there

She felt so much joy
Watching her little boy
Make footprints in the sand
In that lovely beautiful land

Then came waves
Washing them away
The footprints were gone
All in the same day

He made so many memories
While playing around that way
Saving some shells and shiny stones
A treasure one could say.

She was making memories too
Footprints ..she could call her own
To walk along and follow through
Someday when he would be gone
To lands hither ,to her unknown
To make new footprints...of his own.

19. Farewell

Farewell...
The alarm must have gone off early
Like on any other working day.
The morning paper must have been in an embrace
While the cup of tea travelled... up and down
Almost rhythmically...in a daze.

The hurried breakfast
The polished shoes
Some ends tied tight
Some ends still loose
Packing the bag for another day at work
Leaving behind some tunes of hope...
That evening would bring them marching back
From the routine of that everyday track.

The footsteps didn't return.
The tunes will be heard no more.
The shoes were left behind on the steps...
They didn't serve any purpose though...
There were too many bare feet
And so many different shoes
They had travelled onward
Leaving behind shoeless feet.

A journey on the steps became
The last leg of their race
All they left behind was
A quiet, peaceful face.
They'd never go back home
Nor would they ever ring the bell
What seemed like just another day at first
Had become the end of life's journey and thirst.
It's sad to think that maybe...
Someone somewhere regrets
Having been too busy with things mundane;
To have turned around to say Goodbye that day
Though it all now seems in vain...
The thought comes back again and again
Why did it rain....
Why did the rain bring pain.
If there was another chance
She thought
She'd surely say Goodbye
And had she known it might be the last
She'd like to turn back the clock... and fast
And wish the alarm hadn't gone off on time
What had happened that day was beyond reason and
rhyme.
There was no warning of things to come
So many precious lives were lost

And so many dreams must have died too...
The stairway gave way
And brought an end to a journey
For so many simple souls in a day...

20. Nature Supreme

Lovely white lillies
Suddenly -they're here.
At the exact same time
That they'd come last year.
They need no reminder
To know it's time to bloom
In Nature's life cycle
Reminders have no room.

Deep within:
Innate ,inborn, infinite
Nature's endowed with a brilliance
We know nothing about!

What tells the seed to burst open and sprout?
What tells the tiny sapling to stick it's neck out?
What tells the roots to dive deep in?
What tells the leaves to turn a lovely green?

What keeps track of little buds...
What pushes them toward the Sun?
What unfolds each delicate petal

What keeps prodding them on?

To wake up every single day
Most of us need alarms.
To keep schedules in order
Reminders are always up in arms.

Did we let go of that wisdom...
The innate instinct Supreme
And enslave ourselves to
A life mundane,
Run of the mill....indistinct?

There is good reason to believe
Mother Nature is supreme
From buds to blossoms
From seeds to trees.
There's hardly ever a scene
Where alarm bells are needed
To usher them in!

There's a beautiful presence
Which is hard to define
That holds the key
To all that is yours or mine.
Someday let us hope
We can all redeem

The magic that lies
In Nature Supreme.

41

21. Eternal Journey

Every end
Is also a beginning
Of a new journey
Starting afresh .
No sorrow
No pain,no loss no gain.
Dropping into the lap of Mother Earth
Back again ...from where it came
The others will fall off in a day or two
Making way
For the fresh and new
Who knows
The buds that stand tall today
Are fallen flowers from yesterday
Reborn to blossom and bloom again
With little to lose
Even less to gain.

22. The Strange Turn

Nobody bothered-
To see his pain .
The agony that returned-
Again and again.
A long long time had passed.
When one of his close friends had asked-
What's happened to you –you're not the same?
You've really changed .

It happened like this.
With the driving license he had earned-he was thrilled.
The journey of life would be smoother –he believed.
A childhood dream was fulfilled.
As he turned to steer the big truck wheels-
His heart just skipped a beat.
Loaded ,with more than just the goodies
He started his journey home
To meet his lovely daughter and her pretty mom.
That morning she had reminded him-
Come soon today....It's your birthday.
She always made it special-cooking most of his favorite
things.
She gave him much more happiness –than a lot of
money could bring.

By sunset., she was all dressed up .
The kids were ready too-
Papa di gaddi was their dream chariot-
He always gave a ride to the two.

But life's road takes strange unexpected turns.
That evening ,he could not return.
There was a road block-
It used to happen quite often.
The poor man waited –so patiently-
Eying the mobile phone owners –rather enviously.
In the midst of all the traffic and noise-he felt so alone.
If only he could inform the kids,
If only he could reach home.

But we are puppets – and this world is a stage
What will be ,will be he thought..
He did not realize-it was after mid night
That the honking got really loud.
The road was opening ,they heard.
I'll be home soon at last, he thought.
Singing to himself, he set off again.
But it just was not his day.
Now there was a punctured tyre that needed repair.
He did not even have a spare.

Finding help here was rare.
So he trudged along- a long distance-
Before sighting some help.
The night was black-so was his mood.
His wife and kids began to brood.
Why did he break his promise?

At last, he was ready to go.
His state of mind no one else would know.
O God, he thought-
Please take me home
There wait my wife and kids-alone.
Stepping on the gas-full speed he moved-
Waiting to reach his home.

Tired, sleepy-the birthday boy-was on the move again.
Just then –he saw her on the road.
Few inches from his truck.
Before his tired feet could act, the tragedy had struck.
She lay on the road, in a pool of blood-
Lifeless at once-she was dead.

Panicking, he accelerated hard-
Before anyone else could act.
I must get out of here and fast-was all that he could
think.
He had been able to escape.

That was good luck he thought.
But though he reached his home quite soon-
In his heart there was a knot.
Nobody knew what happened –yet his heart was filled
with pain.
The papers said-Truck driver crushes girl and escapes.
Her picture was there.
She was so beautiful-so young ...so fair.

There were tears in his eyes that none could see.
There was a pain in his heart that none could feel.
There was agony-but no one could share.
He stood and stared at the man in the mirror-
Wondering –am I a killer?
In his heart- and in his soul-
The search for the truth is on.
Would they still love him - if they knew-
it was his truck-when tragedy had struck
And he was the man behind the wheel
The day that girl was killed.

Every day-his eyes shed tears.
At night he can not sleep.
His heart still weeps in agony –
Not a single day seems good or sunny
His friends tell him he's looking so old-
His story remains untold.

23. Dearest Ma

Her warm loving hands
Can soothe away all pain
When she's around
There's nothing more to gain.
When we didn't know how to walk
And could barely even talk
When the seas were stormy and rough
Her presence was enough
To help us navigate
Whatever was on the plate.

Now her hair is all silver
And her walk is slow
Measured steps
Take her where she wants to go.
Her soft loving voice
Still sounds the same
She is always cheering us on
As we play life's game.

She is part of all we do
She is always around
For a mother's love and blessings
Are a treasure we have found...

To hold on to forever
Beyond the realms of time
She is the music and the song
And the melody around

Her joys are tied to ours
For she gives with all her heart
Through the days and years that pass
We become her very own part
A bond that brings with it
Unlimited love and grace
My one and only
Dearest Ma ...
I miss your warm embrace.

24. The Lost Traveller

It was still quite dark
When I stepped out for my morning walk
Lost in thought about
What gifts the new day had brought.
Something stirred within
That made me look up
Only to be taken captive
By the view above.
Yes the sky was still very dark
The deepest shade of black
Yet it was telling me a story
In its magnificent ageless glory.
There was the moon,
Crescent as they say
With a veil that made full circle
Decked up with shining stars
Glowing ever so bright in the dark
I looked up and stared for the longest time
Mesmerised ...this show was mine
I had walked in on it alone today
While soundly the others slept away.
Every night and early morning
The show was on for us to see
A glance was all it took

A pause to stop and look
Yet caught up in the web of life
Pulled apart by the strain and strife
We hardly hear the cosmic song
Leave alone stepping up
To join and dance along.
The magic of the moon and stars
Just goes away...once the night has passed.
It is there today
And has been for long
Tuned in majestically
to the cosmic sound.
The secrets of the sky
Await discovery
All it takes is a pause
A glance and then
The stars are ours
As is the moon and the song.

I stood under the beautiful sky
Spellbound,wonderstruck
By what had met my eye
A tinge of regret touched my heart just then
Oh how long had I been missing
This divine vision
That was passing by my side
Every single night

And I was the lost traveller
Was oblivious
Of the sparkling stars
Shining so bright.

25. A necklace of fleeting moments

Chubby cheeks
Tiny chin
No teeth at all
A new life begins.

Long awaited
By family and friends
With the baby's arrival
One phase ends.

A new life begins
As the bundle of joy
Begins a journey
At first treated like a toy.

Days pass
Years fly
In a blink
It's all over and time to die.

Nothing remains constant
For none can capture time
A necklace of fleeting moments

Life is...yours and mine.

53

26. Papa

Papa was a very handsome man
With a beautiful soul to match
His laughter was infectious
One others were bound to catch

He was a loving father
One who nurtured from the start
Leading by example
He knew parenting was an art.

Never an unkind word or gesture
He had a different style
Like a gardener would tend his plants
He helped us grow with a smile

We watched him work day in and out
Giving his best without any doubt
Playing many roles with equal elan
He was like Krishna...a limitless man

He touched many lives
In his life time
Standing tall with those
Who were left behind

He helped everyone
Become their best
And taught us how to balance
Work and rest

Thinking of him and missing him
I wish...he could come around
Just give me one more big bear hug
And share that hearty laughter sound

The mirror seemed to heard my thoughts
For when I looked I found
His nose and eyes and curly hair
Smiling ...in a rebound

Our parents never ever leave us
They walk along our side
Sometimes we cannot see them
Except on the inside.

27. The Unfallen Tear

Her voice is loud
Her words are clear
When she says something
One is bound to hear
Sometimes it is just
Small town talk
What the ladies were discussing
During the evening walk.
Sometimes she shares
Her life's stories
Of joys and sorrows
Fears and pain
What was lost and
What has been gained.
Her eyes don't lie
For when she speaks
They seem to reveal
All that they've seen...
It's been a rather topsy turvy ride
Not always was someone there
By her side.
She laughs a lot
To hide her pain
Else her loneliness

Would drive her insane
The golden days
And moonlit nights
Bring memories old
Of friendly fights
With those who were her family
In her childhood home
That was filled with glee.
She wears a mask
For the world to see
Hiding herself
Like a child behind a tree...
Sometimes,
The words disappear
And her silence is all one can hear
But her eyes still speak
Loud and clear
If only one can tune in
To the unfallen tear.

28. A puddle of water

He was trying to stop her
But she moved like a humming bird
Dodging him once
Then again and again
Till he gave up and said
Go ahead
Do what you can.

She threw off her slippers
And jumped right in
That puddle of water
Was just the thing
She was waiting to jump into
And splash around in

Children and puddles
Have something going
If they ever see one
They just have to go in
Get their soft tiny feet
Wet and then bring
Some water along
To make footprints

Back and forth
Merrily they go
Splashing and moving
With nothing to do
Carefree spirits
Going along with the flow
A puddle of water
What a source of delight
A few footprints and laughter
Can't do any harm...right?

He gave up and watched
Her jumping with glee
A puddle of water and
A spirit that was free
Smiling to himself
He thought he could see
The shadow of a little boy
He wanted to be.

29. Everyone is mine

They thought she wasn't happy
They thought she may be feeling trapped
They looked at her with pity
They agreed she must be very sad

For she was in the house all day
Taking care of everyone's needs
Giving them what they wanted
Ripened fruit or sunflower seeds

She woke up early everyday
When the Sun was still on the way
She cleaned the house ,took bath and prayed
By then the darkness began to fade

She was the lady of the house
And ran it really smooth
They counted on her night and day
She was their anchor all the way

She made the house a home so warm
A place where storms would meet the calm
Waking up to the morning alarm
While the rooster laughed out loud in the farm

She loved them all
And they loved her
She knew they knew
That's how bonds grew

And then years later
When she was old
Her kids had grown up
Big and bold
They cared for her
Like a mother would
The circle had come
Around for good

She had the joy of knowing well
Without having to shout and tell
It's all about choices we make
Some we give and some we take
To each his own
Is the only way
Some sweet some sour
Fill in the day

Not everyone needs to rush around
There's joy within
Waiting to be found

For when life comes
A full circle
Each one will know
It was all a miracle

There's a seamless flow
As we age and grow
Till our minds are ready
To experience and know
Aham brahmasmi
I am Divine
I belong to everyone
Everyone is mine.

30. Reel not real

On the day of Mahashivaratri
He searched with open eyes
For a place where he could buy
Some belpatra and flowers nearby.

She sat there on the ground
Selling some wild fruit and leaves
Knowing how precious they would be
For anyone who believes

The old flowerseller had woken up early
And gone walking barefoot in the wild
To pluck and gather fresh bel leaves
In great demand for the pooja rites

He looked down at her and asked
What was the selling price
Of a few bel leaves and flowers
That would be very important for a few hours

A few rupees ...was all she asked
In exchange for the hard work she had done
Plucking through the thorns and collecting the leaves
She had come to the sell the stuff for the customer's ease.

A while ago he was telling his friend
How pious and helpful he was
And how deeply he often prayed
For world peace at large.

Of how he would always be found
Reaching out to those in need
Helping others was his second nature
Be it any living creature indeed.

Then he spoke aloud and stood there
Trying to strike a bargain
Haggling with the poor old woman
Who already had little to gain

He insisted and forced her
To sell the belpatra cheap
She seemed rather unhappy
Her intense eyes were deep

Just then it rang out loud and clear
The nearby temple's bell...
The celebrations were starting off
As everyone could tell

He held the bag full of bel leaves
Feeling almost triumphant
Because he thought he'd managed to strike
A rather good bargain

The seller was gone,nowhere to be seen
After he had turned around.
It was as if she'd chosen to leave
Stay hidden and not be found

She wasn't looking happy
When he had struck the deal
Where did she go he wondered
For guilt was all he could feel

A thin line stood there
Mocking him
And for a moment he paused
What had he gained by buying cheap
From the old woman with eyes so deep.

Why did he haggle so hard
He heard himself asking
She was just trying to make ends meet
And there he was ...
With a car parked down the street

There is a big difference you know
Between the real and the reel...
For the reels are there to show the world
Minus the human feel
It is so easy to forget
But hands and hearts can tell
The real deal...lies far beyond
The sound of the temple bell.

31. A Mother's Treasure

He ran to her and smiled sweetly
Looking up at her from her knees
Ma close your eyes ,he said
And put out your hand please.
She did as she was told
And saw the magic unfold.
'Open your eyes
See what I got for you'
The little boy said excitedly
'Look what I found
Near that tall big tree
You will be so very
Proud of me'.
One by one he put them out
Gently on her palm.
Colourful shiny pebbles
Which while playing he had found.
She looked at him and smiled lovingly
At the pebbles,
Some rough some perfectly round.
'Do you think it's a king's treasure
Which was hidden in the ground?'
Her eyes filled up her heart melted
She didn't know what to say

Sometimes there are moments
When silence wins the day.
What would a king know she thought to herself
About treasure which he'd brought
For it would take a mother's heart
To know what it was worth.

32. Invisible Bond

With folded hands
Heads bowed in gratitude
The old lady and her son
In front of the temple stood.
She was smiling
So was he
If you saw their faces
You'd think they were wealthy.
They had brought flowers to sell
And pooja samagri
Wanting to return home
A little early.
A young couple had come
To celebrate their special day
And saw the old mother and son
Sitting along the way.
They bought all her flowers and samagri
And even touched her feet
She reminded them of their Ma they said
Whom they could no longer meet
For she had left the world behind
And was now united with the Divine.
She showered them with blessings

And spoke with love from her heart
A bond invisible seems to bind
Which those who seek...will surely find.

33. The Flight

The moon was shining through the leaves
Moving along the pitch black sky
The day had gone and it was time
Homeward ,for the birds to fly.
The cool soft air
Touched her silver hair
Her wrinkled hands were cold
She was beginning to wonder
If she was growing old.
When a voice she heard
Came from deep within
And gave her wings to fly
You were not born
Nor will you die
It's an illusion of the eye
For that which was and will always be
Is the truth...waiting to be found
It's the body that will wither and die
Your soul is eternal...free to fly
Soaring beyond
Embracing the sky.

34. Birth

Their eyes met
And in that fleeting moment
They shared a universe.
She was the mother who just gave birth
And he was a father now
Life had been a painful wait
They'd been married for years
Ten plus eight.
They longed to hold
A baby their own
So many little kids they knew
Were now older and grown.
Life seemed unfair
Barren and bare
Despite everything...their love endured
They held on together
And shared a dream.
Now she was here
Their bundle of joy
Precious and pure
A blessing for sure
Their eyes were locked
As they saw it all
The journey they had lived

Through the spring and fall.
Someday
She would be grown up and tall....
Not knowing how precious she was
For the mother who had waited
So many years
And the father
Who'd never let a tear fall.
They come and find a home their own
And give birth to someone too
For a mother and a father grow
Through experiences they never knew...
Would change them and the life they live
A baby is born and gives birth too
To a father and mother
Just as new.

35. A Green blade of Grass

74

Standing alone
Reaching out to the sky
Living life to the fullest
Not afraid to die
Knowing fully well
That a time will come
When a shade of brown
The deep green will become
Till then
The tiny little blade of grass
Would embrace what was
Knowing fully well
That which comes
Shall pass.

36. Whither roots

This happened indoor
On a cosy winter day
At the vegetable store
That had a sparkling clean floor.
People were pushing to lay their hands
On the leafy greens stacked up on the stands.
I looked up and saw
A poster on the wall
'Please do not break off the roots
Of any vegetables at all.'
It was meant to convey a message clear
The weight of the roots ,the buyers had to bear.
The mother took her quickly
To a corner of the store
And told her young daughter -
Oh come on be quick
Just break off the roots and throw them
Nobody will come to know.
She looked a little sheepish
And red in the face too
Perhaps a bit embarassed
Of what mother was asking her to do.
She picked up a big bundle
Of green coriander leaves

And broke off the roots
As fast as she could.
Very pleased
The mother smiled
Didn't I say it would be easy?
Cutting through
The customer queue
They paid off the bill quickly
And in no time , were out of sight
Having blurred the line ,between the wrong and right.
On the clean store floor,the broken roots lay
Because that mother cut corners...not wanting to pay.
You can go to a quiet corner
Break off the muddy roots
You can pay a quarter less
You can step on someone's boots
Yet
If this is what we teach our kids
What right have we to complain...
When they come back and do the same
It'll be a loss with nothing to gain.
Here was a mother trying to teach
Her own young daughter...how to cheat...

Little wonder we're living in a world
Where values have lost their sheen
For who is teaching little ones

To be gentle and kind ,not mean?

Nipped in the bud ,
how would anyone learn
The values of strong roots...
If mothers were to teach their kids
To step on someone's boots?

So this where the story ends
And a new one begins...
Hoping no one one will have to ask...
Whither roots...
Again.

37. One Moment

One moment he could have heard the raindrops falling
The next moment
He realised he was deaf.
One moment she was holding him close to her heart
The next moment
He was lying dead in the dirt.
One moment he was wearing his brand new shoes
The next moment
His feet were gone.
One moment she was holding the fruit filled bag
The next moment
Only the bag remained.
One moment they were waiting to get justice
The next moment ,everything was blown.
His white beard could not hide his tears
She couldn't find a voice for her worst fears
In the flash of a moment
Many lives turned upside down
There was a bomb blast in that part of town.
God knows for what their blood was shed
Innocent people,who were now dead.
A tragedy that was manmade
Had changed so many lives
Left behind such loss and pain

Giving rise to a question again:
How could anyone have
Something ,from that ,to gain?
Perhaps we should let
Our children run the world
And with pure hearts and hands
Build happy peaceful lands.

38. Stars

Have you ever seen the stars shine in bright sunlight?
Of course not.
They shine when its dark...they shine at night.
Darkness has a purpose too
It reveals the shiny stars to you.
The Master who made the stars in the sky
Sure enough put a few in the human eye
This morning I realised
There's a purpose in the darkness we sometimes find in
life
That it comes forth to bring home the stars
That lie within our being...close to our hearts.

I just hope when the darkness lifts and the night has
gone
The memory of the shining stars will linger on....

39. Wheels of Life

Today I saw the short summary
Of milestones of life's entire journey
Walking alone around the park
Just before it became too dark
When the two went past in slow motion
A wheelchair driver...with an old patient.
The escort was constantly on the phone
Speaking to someone else he must have known
And sitting timidly with his head bent down
Was the old man ...staring blankly at the ground.
He wore golden glasses
That must 've seen a better world
His wrinkled hands sat quietly
Like a long story waiting to be told
They must have seen much better days
That had now sadly parted ways.
As if it was meant to be
A lesson of time's infirmity
Just when wheelchair left with the old man
Entered a couple with a baby in a pram .
How joyful they looked together I saw
A perfect picture...without a flaw
It all flashed before me like a magical scene
What is ,what was ,what must have been.

40. Words

82

Harsh words can wound the soul
Kind words can heal
Words have the power
To determine how you feel

So choose to use
Kind happy words
Speak well to all you know
For words can leave a footprint
Everywhere you go

So when you speak
Be wise and sure
To use kind words
Polite and pure
'Cos even when you're far away
You words can impact someone's day.

www.ingramcontent.com/pod-product-compliance
Lightning Source LLC
LaVergne TN
LVHW010019200726
843495LV00015B/1831